BRIDGE TECHNIQUE SERIES

ELIMINATIONS

& THROW INS

David Bird • Marc Smith

MASTER POINT PRESS • TORONTO

Master Point Press
331 Douglas Ave
Toronto, Ontario, Canada
M5M 1H2
(416) 781-0351   Internet www.masterpointpress.com

Distributed in the USA by Barricade Books
150 Fifth Avenue, Suite 700
New York, NY 10011
(800) 59-BOOKS

Canadian Cataloguing in Publication Data
Bird, David, 1946-
Eliminations & throw-ins

(Bridge technique; 4)
ISBN 1-894154-24-X

1. Contract bridge - Dummy plays. I. Smith, Marc, 1960- . II Title.
III. Eliminations and throw ins. IV Series: Bird, David, 1946-.
Bridge technique; 4

GV1282.435 B733 2000   795. 41'.53   C00-931333-8

Cover design and Interior: Olena S. Sullivan
Editor: Ray Lee

Printed and bound in Canada

1 2 3 4 5 6 7   07 06 05 04 03 02 01 00

Contents

Bridge Technique Series

Available Now

Entry Management

Tricks with Trumps

Safety Plays

Eliminations and Throw-Ins

Deceptive Card Play

Planning in Suit Contracts

Available March, 2001

Planning in Notrump Contracts

Defensive Signaling

Squeezes for Everyone

Available September, 2001

Planning in Defense

Reading the Cards

Tricks with Finesses

CHAPTER 1

Basics of Elimination Play

It is never to your advantage to make the first play in a suit — this is a fundamental fact of cardplay. You will always fare at least as well, usually better, if the opponents open the suit. Look at these typical holdings:

1.　　◇ Q 7 6　　　**2.**　　♡ J 10 6　　　**3.**　　♠ 8 4 2

```
   N                 N                 N
 W   E             W   E             W   E
   S                 S                 S
```

　　◇ J 8 5　　　　　　♡ A 5 2　　　　　♠ K 6 3

If you have to play combination (1) yourself, the best chance is to lead towards one honor, then towards the other. Your main hope is that the ace and king are in the same hand. If the opponents open the suit instead, you are certain to score a trick.

Tackle position (2) yourself and the chance of two tricks is remote. When a defender has to make the first play, it soars to more than 75%. Indeed, if East has to make the first play and West has to return the suit, you are certain of two tricks.

Play combination (3) yourself and you are likely to score a trick only when East holds the ace. If instead you can force West to lead the suit, a trick is certain.

So, we're agreed. You would like the defenders to make the first play in your key suit — the one where you are worried about too many losers. How can you force them to do this? When you have plenty of trumps in both hands it can be quite easy. You throw the lead to a defender at a time when he cannot safely lead any suit but the one you want him to play. Let's see a full deal involving the diamond position shown in (1) above:

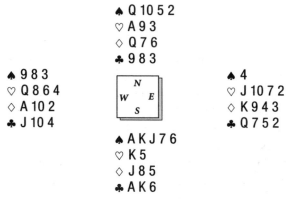

♠ Q 10 5 2
♡ A 9 3
◇ Q 7 6
♣ 9 8 3

♠ 9 8 3
♡ Q 8 6 4
◇ A 10 2
♣ J 10 4

♠ 4
♡ J 10 7 2
◇ K 9 4 3
♣ Q 7 5 2

♠ A K J 7 6
♡ K 5
◇ J 8 5
♣ A K 6

West leads a trump against 4♠ and you draw trumps. You have a certain loser in clubs and must therefore restrict your diamond losers to two. The best way of achieving this is to force the defenders to make the first play in diamonds.

What will happen if you play ace, king and a third club, immediately after drawing trumps? No good. The defender who wins will be able to exit safely in hearts, leaving you to open the diamond suit.

Before throwing the defenders on lead, you must remove the defenders' safe exit in the heart suit. Cash the ♡K, cross to the ♡A, and ruff a heart. You have 'eliminated' the heart suit — the defenders will not now be able to play a heart without conceding a ruff-and-discard.

Now you turn to the clubs. The third round of the suit not only passes the lead to one of the defenders, it also eliminates the clubs from both your hand and the dummy. This will be the position:

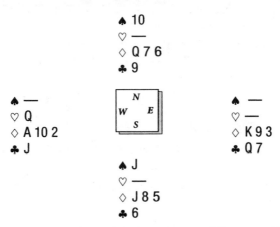

♠ 10
♡ —
♢ Q 7 6
♣ 9

♠ —
♡ Q
♢ A 10 2
♣ J

♠ —
♡ —
♢ K 9 3
♣ Q 7

♠ J
♡ —
♢ J 8 5
♣ 6

When you exit with a club, it makes no difference which defender wins the trick. He will have to open the diamond suit or give you a ruff-and-discard (allowing you to ruff in one hand and throw a diamond from the other). You will lose just one club and two diamonds.

Note how important it was for you to have at least one trump in each hand when you threw the defenders on lead. If the ruff-and-discard element had not been present, they could have exited safely in one of the suits that you had eliminated.

Opportunities for 'Elimination Play', as it is called, are very frequent and will arise nearly every time you come to the table. Any time you spend in learning how to execute such plays, and how to defend against them, will be amply rewarded.

Key Points

1. Look for an elimination play when you have plenty of trumps in both hands. The aim is to force the defenders to make the first play in your key suit.

2. To perform an elimination play: draw trumps, eliminate the suits where the defenders can exit safely, then throw them in. They will have to lead your key suit or concede a ruff-and-discard.

3. For an elimination ending to succeed, you need at least one trump both in your hand and in the dummy.

Different Forms of Elimination Play

In order to perform a 'throw-in' you need an exit card. When your exit card is in the suit the defenders have led, you may have to plan your play well in advance. Look at this slam deal:

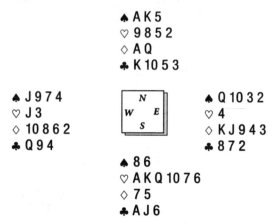

```
              ♠ A K 5
              ♡ 9 8 5 2
              ◇ A Q
              ♣ K 10 5 3

  ♠ J 9 7 4      N          ♠ Q 10 3 2
  ♡ J 3      W       E      ♡ 4
  ◇ 10 8 6 2     S          ◇ K J 9 4 3
  ♣ Q 9 4                   ♣ 8 7 2

              ♠ 8 6
              ♡ A K Q 10 7 6
              ◇ 7 5
              ♣ A J 6
```

West leads the ◇2 against 6♡. At least half the players on the planet, probably more, would play the queen from dummy. The finesse would lose and East would exit safely. The success of the contract would then depend on declarer's guessing skills in clubs.

When you're familiar with elimination play, you can claim the contract the moment dummy goes down! You win the first trick with the

◇A, draw trumps, and eliminate the spade suit (cashing the ace and king and ruffing the third round). These cards remain:

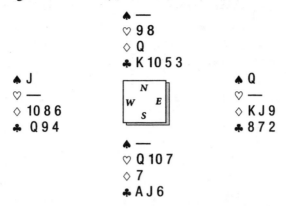

```
                    ♠ —
                    ♡ 9 8
                    ◇ Q
                    ♣ K 10 5 3
  ♠ J                              ♠ Q
  ♡ —              N               ♡ —
  ◇ 10 8 6      W     E            ◇ K J 9
  ♣ Q 9 4          S               ♣ 8 7 2
                    ♠ —
                    ♡ Q 10 7
                    ◇ 7
                    ♣ A J 6
```

Now you exit in diamonds. It makes no difference which defender wins with the king. He will have to play a club, removing the guess in that suit, or give a ruff-and-discard, allowing you to throw a club from the South hand.

Two or more losers in the exit suit

Suppose your holdings in the exit suit are A-x-x and x-x-x. It makes no difference that the opponents will be able to cash a second winner in this suit. They will still be faced with the familiar dilemma thereafter: to open your key suit or to concede a ruff-and-discard.

On the next deal, you have three potential losers in the exit suit:

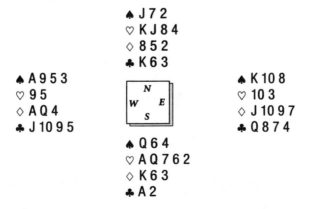

```
                    ♠ J 7 2
                    ♡ K J 8 4
                    ◇ 8 5 2
                    ♣ K 6 3
  ♠ A 9 5 3                        ♠ K 10 8
  ♡ 9 5            N               ♡ 10 3
  ◇ A Q 4       W     E            ◇ J 10 9 7
  ♣ J 10 9 5       S               ♣ Q 8 7 4
                    ♠ Q 6 4
                    ♡ A Q 7 6 2
                    ◇ K 6 3
                    ♣ A 2
```

You buy the contract in a modest 2♡ and West leads the ♣J. You draw trumps and eliminate the clubs. What next?

Suppose you decide to play on spades. However you manipulate your spade honors, you will go down. You will lose three spade tricks and three diamonds.

To guarantee the contract, you must exit in diamonds. A diamond to the king loses, and the defenders score two more tricks in the suit. That's the end of the road for them. They will have to open the spade suit, giving you a winner there, or concede a ruff-and-discard. You would play the contract the same way with three small diamonds in each hand.

Exiting in the trump suit

When the only outstanding trump is a master, it is not normally beneficial to declarer to play a further round of the suit. In an elimination situation however, it may be the only way to make the contract. The defender thrown on lead with the master trump may have to give you a trick. Take a look at this deal:

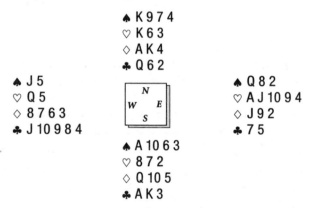

♠ K 9 7 4
♥ K 6 3
♦ A K 4
♣ Q 6 2

♠ J 5   ♠ Q 8 2
♥ Q 5   ♥ A J 10 9 4
♦ 8 7 6 3   ♦ J 9 2
♣ J 10 9 8 4   ♣ 7 5

♠ A 10 6 3
♥ 8 7 2
♦ Q 10 5
♣ A K 3

A heart lead would have beaten your contract of 4♠ but West starts with the ♣J. How would you play the hand?

You win the club lead and play two rounds of trumps, pleased to see the suit break 3-2. If you play on hearts yourself, you will need West to hold the ace. A better idea is to force East to open the heart suit, which may be possible if he holds the missing trump.

After three rounds of diamonds, eliminating that suit, you play on clubs. East is welcome to ruff the third round because he would then have to play hearts, allowing dummy's king to score. If East declines to ruff the third club, you will throw him in with a trump — to the same effect.

Note how important it was to play the minor suits in the right order. If you had played on clubs before diamonds, East would have ruffed the third round and exited safely with a diamond. One down! West's opening lead of the ♣J was probably from a sequence. This suggested that West would hold length in the suit, leaving East with a potential shortage.

The prospect of gaining a trick by exiting in trumps may affect the way you play the trump suit itself. Look at this deal:

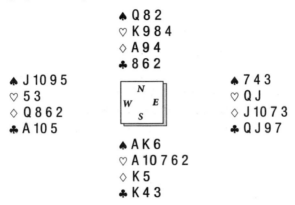

```
                    ♠ Q 8 2
                    ♡ K 9 8 4
                    ◇ A 9 4
                    ♣ 8 6 2
  ♠ J 10 9 5                        ♠ 7 4 3
  ♡ 5 3          ┌──────────┐       ♡ Q J
  ◇ Q 8 6 2      │    N     │       ◇ J 10 7 3
  ♣ A 10 5       │ W     E  │       ♣ Q J 9 7
                 │    S     │
                 └──────────┘
                    ♠ A K 6
                    ♡ A 10 7 6 2
                    ◇ K 5
                    ♣ K 4 3
```

You reach 4♡ and West leads the ♠J, won in the South hand. You cash the ace of trumps and East follows with the jack (or queen). What next?

The Principle of Restricted Choice states that East's honor is almost twice as likely to be a singleton as to be a chosen card from Q-J doubleton. So, looking at the trump suit in isolation, the best play by a good margin is to finesse dummy's nine on the second round. On this particular hand, though, this would lead to defeat. East would win and switch to clubs — one down!

You can guarantee your contract by rising with the ♡K on the second round. Why is that? Because if East does show out, as you expect, you can endplay West later. You will eliminate the diamonds and spades, then throw him in with his high trump. He will have to open the clubs or give you a ruff-and-discard.

When the cards lie as in the diagram, rising with the king of trumps is immediately successful — you bring in the trump suit without loss. Playing in this fashion, you will make the contract whichever defender holds the missing trump honor.

The defenders have to play the key suit twice

When there is only one suit that the defenders can play, without conceding a ruff-and-discard, they will have to continue playing this suit as long as they retain the lead. Suppose you have eliminated the other three suits and the defenders are forced to play on diamonds here:

$\diamondsuit$ J 10 3

$\diamondsuit$ K Q 7 2 | N / W E / S | $\diamondsuit$ 9 8 4

$\diamondsuit$ A 6 5

If East is on lead, he can play a diamond to his partner's queen. No damage has been done yet but West must now play the suit again. You will score two diamond tricks however the suit lies.

Here is a full deal involving this diamond suit:

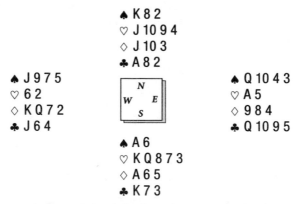

♠ K 8 2
♡ J 10 9 4
◇ J 10 3
♣ A 8 2

♠ J 9 7 5
♡ 6 2
◇ K Q 7 2
♣ J 6 4

♠ Q 10 4 3
♡ A 5
◇ 9 8 4
♣ Q 10 9 5

♠ A 6
♡ K Q 8 7 3
◇ A 6 5
♣ K 7 3

You reach 4♡ and the defenders play two rounds of trumps. How will you tackle the play?

With plenty of trumps in both hands, it is natural to consider an elimination. You remove the spades from the scene, then play ace, king and another club. The defenders can choose who wins the third club but it will make no difference. Say East wins. He plays a diamond and West wins with the queen. He is now endplayed and the game is made.

No guess of any sort was required on that hand; you could have claimed the contract after Trick 2 (when East failed to find the killing diamond switch). Sometimes you will have a guess to make on the second round of the key suit. Suppose West has to open this spade suit:

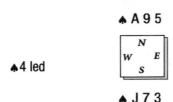

♠ A 9 5

♠4 led

♠ J 7 3

West leads the ♠4 and you play low, East winning with the king or queen. When he returns a low spade you will have to guess whether to play the jack (hoping that East started with both high honors) or to play low (hoping that East holds the ten and West will have to play the remaining high honor). Which do you think is the better proposition?

It is better, by a factor of 2-to-1, to play low from hand. The Principle of Restricted Choice states that East is more likely to have played his high honor because he had to (it was the only card that would beat the jack) rather than because he chose it from two equal cards.

If you find this difficult to accept, look at it this way. Your play from hand makes a difference only when East holds precisely two of the three missing honors (K, Q and 10). For every 300 deals on which East does hold two honors he will hold:

K Q	100 times
K 10	100 times
Q 10	100 times

So, if you always play low from the hand on the return — whichever honor East played on the first round — you will succeed 200 times out of 300. If you rise with your jack, you will succeed only 100 times. There are many, many bridge players who go to their deathbeds still not believing in Restricted Choice. Don't be one of them! The odds will be 2-to-1 in your favor whenever you play against such people.

Exiting in the key suit

So far, you have exited in one suit and forced the defenders to play on another. An equally common form of elimination play involves exiting in the key suit itself. Before we look at some of the holdings where this may be profitable, let's see the play in the context of a whole deal:

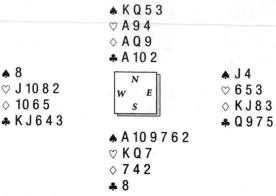

```
              ♠ K Q 5 3
              ♡ A 9 4
              ◇ A Q 9
              ♣ A 10 2
♠ 8                            ♠ J 4
♡ J 10 8 2       N             ♡ 6 5 3
◇ 10 6 5     W       E         ◇ K J 8 3
♣ K J 6 4 3      S             ♣ Q 9 7 5
              ♠ A 10 9 7 6 2
              ♡ K Q 7
              ◇ 7 4 2
              ♣ 8
```

West leads the ♡J against your contract of 4♠. You win with the king, draw trumps in two rounds, then eliminate the clubs and the hearts. The lead is in the South hand and these cards remain:

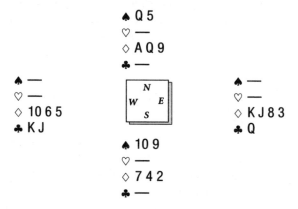

```
              ♠ Q 5
              ♡ —
              ◇ A Q 9
              ♣ —
♠ —                            ♠ —
♡ —              N             ♡ —
◇ 10 6 5     W       E         ◇ K J 8 3
♣ K J           S             ♣ Q
              ♠ 10 9
              ♡ —
              ◇ 7 4 2
              ♣ —
```

The time has come to exit in the key suit itself. You lead a diamond and insert dummy's nine. East wins with the jack and has to return a diamond into the A-Q (or concede a you-know-what). Note that it would not help West to insert the ten on the first round of diamonds. You would cover with dummy's queen, taken with the king, and East would have to lead from his jack into the A-9 tenace.

There are many similar positions:

```
                 ♡ A J 10
                    N
♡ 9 6 3        W        E        ♡ K Q 5 4
                    S
                 ♡ 8 7 2
```

You finesse the jack or ten. East wins and must lead into the tenace.

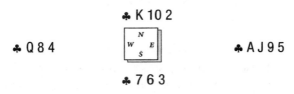

The best chance with this holding is to finesse the nine. When West holds the ten, East will win with an honor and have to lead into the A-J tenace.

With all other side suits eliminated, you lead a club to the ten. East wins and has to concede a trick. Once again it would serve no purpose for West to play high, inserting the queen.

$$\diamond\ Q\ J\ 3$$

$\diamond\ 9\ 7\ 4$ [N W E S] $\diamond\ A\ K\ 10\ 8$

$$\diamond\ 6\ 5\ 2$$

A diamond to the queen and king forces East to concede a trick.

In each of the last four positions, declarer could not achieve an extra trick unless the key suit was played in an elimination situation (where the defenders would have to play a second round of the suit after winning the first).

Elimination play can sometimes protect you against a bad break. Look at the club suit here:

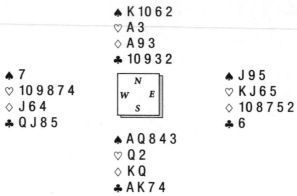

♠ K 10 6 2
♥ A 3
♦ A 9 3
♣ 10 9 3 2

♠ 7
♥ 10 9 8 7 4
♦ J 6 4
♣ Q J 8 5

♠ J 9 5
♥ K J 6 5
♦ 10 8 7 5 2
♣ 6

♠ A Q 8 4 3
♥ Q 2
♦ K Q
♣ A K 7 4

You reach 6♠ and West places the ♥10 on the table. Since you have a discard available on the diamond suit, you are not tempted to run the lead to your queen. You rise with dummy's ♥A, draw two rounds of trumps, and cash the diamond honors in your hand. You then cross to dummy with a third round of trumps and play the ♦A, throwing your heart loser. A heart ruff eliminates that suit and all now depends on avoiding two losers in the club suit. Any ideas?

Playing ace, king and another club will lead to a sad end. The winning play, proof against any lie of the club suit, is to play the ace of clubs followed by a low club. If either defender began with Q-J-x-x he will be endplayed after winning the second round.

The same play would succeed here:

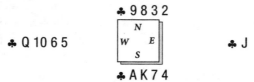

♣ 9 8 3 2

♣ Q 10 6 5

♣ J

♣ A K 7 4

Once the ace draws an honor (from either side), a low club to the 9-8 will guarantee the contract.

Two key suits

Until now, we have considered hands with only one key suit. This is usually the case, but occasionally the defender thrown on lead will be forced to concede a trick in one of two suits. With this clue in mind, see if you can spot the winning play here:

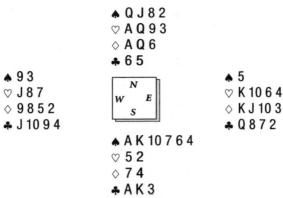

```
                    ♠ Q J 8 2
                    ♡ A Q 9 3
                    ◇ A Q 6
                    ♣ 6 5
♠ 9 3                              ♠ 5
♡ J 8 7         N                 ♡ K 10 6 4
◇ 9 8 5 2    W     E              ◇ K J 10 3
♣ J 10 9 4         S              ♣ Q 8 7 2
                    ♠ A K 10 7 6 4
                    ♡ 5 2
                    ◇ 7 4
                    ♣ A K 3
```

A sparkling auction carries you to 6♠ and you have no cause to complain when West leads the ♣J. How should you play the hand?

Win the club lead, draw one round of trumps, then cash the remaining club honor and ruff a club high. Next, return to your hand with a second round of trumps. Which red-suit queen should you finesse first, do you think?

The answer is neither! If you do finesse one of the queens, East will win and exit safely in the same suit. You will then have to take the other finesse, tumbling to defeat. The winning line is to play a low heart to the nine. East wins with the ten but will then have to give you a twelfth trick by leading into one or other A-Q tenace (or playing a club, which will give a ruff-and-discard).

Extra chance via elimination play

Some elimination plays guarantee the success of a contract; others merely improve the chances. Look at this deal, for example:

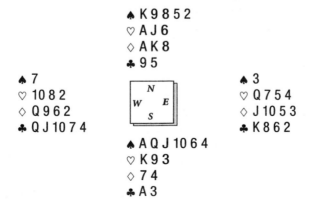

```
                    ♠ K 9 8 5 2
                    ♡ A J 6
                    ◇ A K 8
                    ♣ 9 5
♠ 7                                ♠ 3
♡ 10 8 2        N                  ♡ Q 7 5 4
◇ Q 9 6 2    W     E               ◇ J 10 5 3
♣ Q J 10 7 4       S              ♣ K 8 6 2
                    ♠ A Q J 10 6 4
                    ♡ K 9 3
                    ◇ 7 4
                    ♣ A 3
```

West leads the ♣Q against 6♠. You cannot avoid losing a club and if you play hearts yourself, you will need West to hold the queen. Elimination play provides you with an extra chance. Do you see how?

Win the club lead, draw trumps, and eliminate the diamonds. You then exit in clubs. If East wins, he must surrender the contract. If West wins, he will have to play a heart, giving you a double chance in the suit. By running his heart lead to your hand, you will make twelve tricks when West holds the ten (as in the diagram). If East produces the ten, your original chance of finessing dummy's jack is still intact.

See if you can spot the extra chance on the next deal:

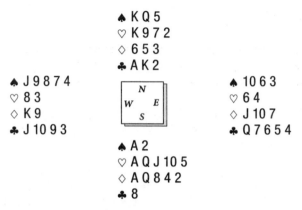

```
              ♠ K Q 5
              ♡ K 9 7 2
              ◇ 6 5 3
              ♣ A K 2
♠ J 9 8 7 4                    ♠ 10 6 3
♡ 8 3          N               ♡ 6 4
◇ K 9       W     E            ◇ J 10 7
♣ J 10 9 3     S               ♣ Q 7 6 5 4
              ♠ A 2
              ♡ A Q J 10 5
              ◇ A Q 8 4 2
              ♣ 8
```

West leads the ♣J against 6♡. You draw trumps and eliminate the clubs and spades. The lead is in dummy and these cards remain:

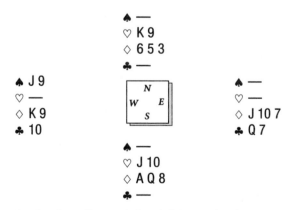

```
              ♠ —
              ♡ K 9
              ◇ 6 5 3
              ♣ —
♠ J 9                          ♠ —
♡ —            N               ♡ —
◇ K 9       W     E            ◇ J 10 7
♣ 10           S               ♣ Q 7
              ♠ —
              ♡ J 10
              ◇ A Q 8
              ♣ —
```

You lead a low diamond from dummy, hoping to see the seven appear from East. You would then be able to cover with the eight and claim the contract. No, East is aware of the situation and rises with the

♢J. If you finesse the queen, you will go down. West will win and exit safely with another diamond.

To give yourself the best chance, you must rise with the ace of diamonds and return to dummy with a trump. You lead a second round of diamonds and only now do you play the queen. West wins but... your luck is in. He has no more diamonds and must give you a ruff-and-discard. You would still make the contact if East held the ♢K, of course. Elimination play gave you the extra chance of West holding king doubleton.

Key points

1. Once you have prepared for an elimination there are many ways to throw the defenders on lead. You can exit with a trump, in a side suit (with one or more losers), or in the key suit itself.

2. While the defenders retain the lead they will have to play on the key suit (or concede a ruff-and-discard). It is often the second play in the key suit that surrenders a trick

A.

 ♠ A J 7 3
 ♡ K 7 6
 ◇ A 10 4
 ♣ K 9 6

♣Q led

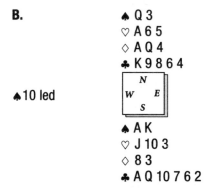

 ♠ K Q 10 6 5
 ♡ J 5 2
 ◇ K 8 3
 ♣ A 3

You reach 4♠ and West leads the ♣Q. How will you play the hand? (Aim for a more comprehensive answer than 'Elimination Play'!)

B.

 ♠ Q 3
 ♡ A 6 5
 ◇ A Q 4
 ♣ K 9 8 6 4

♠10 led

 ♠ A K
 ♡ J 10 3
 ◇ 8 3
 ♣ A Q 10 7 6 2

Playing in a Pairs event, you bypass the high-scoring 3NT contract and then feel you have to try for 6♣ rather than 5♣. How will you tackle this ambitious contract after West leads the ♠10?

C.

♠ Q 9 6 4
♡ A 5
◇ K Q 9
♣ A K 8 4

♡8 led

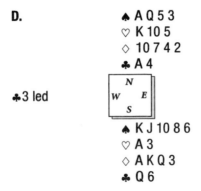

♠ A K J 10 2
♡ Q 9
◇ A J 4
♣ J 10 3

You reach 6♠ and West finds the one lead to trouble you —
a heart. How will you play the hand?

D.

♠ A Q 5 3
♡ K 10 5
◇ 10 7 4 2
♣ A 4

♣3 led

♠ K J 10 8 6
♡ A 3
◇ A K Q 3
♣ Q 6

You reach 6♠ and West leads the ♣3. How will you play the
hand? (Trumps are 3-1.)

Answers

A. If you play on hearts yourself, finding that the ace and queen are both poorly placed, you are likely to lose three hearts and a diamond. A better idea is to force the defenders to play on hearts first. You should win the club lead, draw trumps, and eliminate the club suit. You can then play three rounds of diamonds. Whichever defender wins the third diamond, he will not be able to play on hearts without giving you a trick.

B. Win the spade lead, draw trumps, and take the diamond finesse. When this succeeds, you are over the first hurdle. You cash the ace of diamonds and ruff dummy's last diamond, eliminating the suit. After cashing the remaining spade honor, you cross to dummy with a trump and lead a low heart towards the jack (exiting in the key suit itself). When the king and queen of hearts lie with the same defender, he will be endplayed — forced to give you a second heart trick. You will succeed also if East mistakenly wins with the king from K-x or K-x-x.

C. It is most unlikely that the ♡8 lead has been made away from the king. You should rise with the ♡A, draw trumps, and eliminate the diamonds. You can then exit in hearts. If East wins, as you expect, he will have to lead a club (ending your problems in that suit) or give you a ruff-and-discard.

D. There is a fair chance that West has led away from the ♣K. However, it would be a needless risk to run the lead to your queen. You might then go down if diamonds broke 4-1. Win the club lead with the ace, draw trumps, and eliminate the heart suit. You then cash two top diamonds. Even if a defender started with ◇J-x-x-x, you are still safe. You exit with a club. The defender who wins will either have to lead away from the ◇J or (if he was the one short in diamonds) give you a ruff-and-discard.

CHAPTER 3

Loser-on-Loser Play

On most of the hands we have seen so far, it did not matter which defender was given the lead. Suppose, however, that the key suit is one of these:

◇ 7 6 3

```
  N
W   E
  S
```

◇ K 8 2

♡ 8 5 3

```
  N
W   E
  S
```

♡ A Q 6

There's not much point in throwing East in to lead in either of these cases, is there? Forcing East to open these combinations is no better than leading the suit yourself from the dummy. You need to have West on lead in these situations.

One particular type of elimination play allows you to throw in a chosen defender. At the moment of the throw-in, you lead a loser from one hand and — rather than ruffing — discard a loser from the other. The play gains because the defender you throw in will have to give you a trick. It's a complex idea, which will become clearer if we see an example. Here is one that involves the diamond holding above:

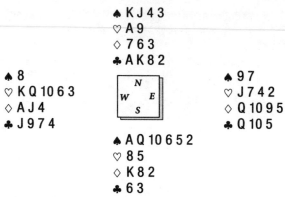

♠ K J 4 3
♡ A 9
◇ 7 6 3
♣ A K 8 2

♠ 8
♡ K Q 10 6 3
◇ A J 4
♣ J 9 7 4

♠ 9 7
♡ J 7 4 2
◇ Q 10 9 5
♣ Q 10 5

♠ A Q 10 6 5 2
♡ 8 5
◇ K 8 2
♣ 6 3

West leads the ♡K against 4♠. Since it will not suit you for East to gain the lead and play through your ◇K, you duck the opening lead. West continues with another heart, won in the dummy. What now?

It will not be good enough to eliminate the clubs, draw trumps, and lead a diamond from dummy. East will insert the ten or the nine and you will lose three diamond tricks. A better idea is to hope that West holds at least four clubs and can be endplayed in the suit.

You win the second round of hearts, draw trumps in two rounds, then cash the two top clubs. When you ruff a third round of clubs, both defenders follow. A third round of trumps returns the lead to dummy and this position has been reached:

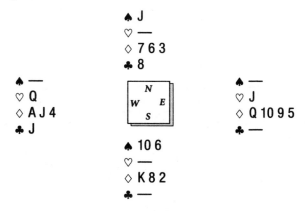

♠ J
♡ —
◇ 7 6 3
♣ 8

♠ —
♡ Q
◇ A J 4
♣ J

♠ —
♡ J
◇ Q 10 9 5
♣ —

♠ 10 6
♡ —
◇ K 8 2
♣ —

You now lead the ♣8 from dummy. When East discards, the contract is guaranteed. You throw a diamond from the South hand, playing one loser on another. West has to win the trick and must then play a diamond from the ace or give you a ruff-and-discard.

Nothing much would be lost if it was East who produced the last club. You could discard a diamond anyway, forcing him to play a diamond. You would be back to your original chance that East held the diamond ace.

Try one of these plays for yourself. Entries to dummy are limited and you will have to play accurately from the start.

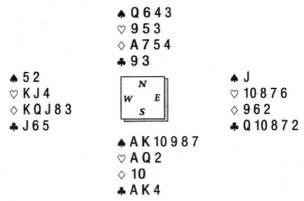

You bid to a small slam in spades and West leads the ◇K, won in the dummy. How would you tackle the play?

All will be well if the ♡K is onside, but it is natural to seek a line that will render the finesse unnecessary. This can be done if West has at least five diamonds — not at all unlikely after the opening lead. You must aim to endplay him on the fourth round of diamonds.

Since entries to dummy are limited, ruff a diamond at Trick 2. After drawing trumps with the ace and queen, you ruff a second diamond. When you cash the two top clubs and ruff a club, these cards remain:

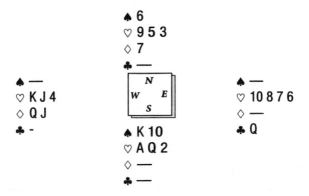

You lead the ◇7 from dummy and discard a heart from your hand, playing a loser on a loser. West wins the trick and is endplayed.

In our first two examples of loser-on-loser play, a particular defender had to win the key trick because his partner had no more cards in the suit. Sometimes, possession of a high card or two will force a particular defender to win. For example, you might have a diamond side suit like this:

◇ A 10 3

◇ Q J 7 6   ◇ 9 8 5 2

◇ K 4

If you need to throw West in, three rounds of diamonds will achieve this whenever West holds both the missing honors.

On the next deal, the West's bidding helps you to place the cards.

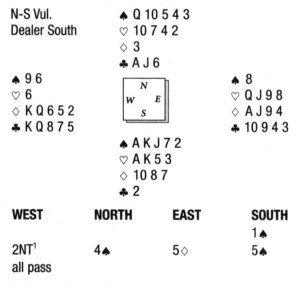

N-S Vul.   ♠ Q 10 5 4 3
Dealer South   ♡ 10 7 4 2
                  ◇ 3
                  ♣ A J 6

♠ 9 6   ♠ 8
♡ 6   ♡ Q J 9 8
◇ K Q 6 5 2   ◇ A J 9 4
♣ K Q 8 7 5   ♣ 10 9 4 3

                  ♠ A K J 7 2
                  ♡ A K 5 3
                  ◇ 10 8 7
                  ♣ 2

WEST	NORTH	EAST	SOUTH
			1♠
2NT[1]	4♠	5◇	5♠
all pass			

1. Unusual Notrump, both minors.

Placing his partner with short diamonds, South decided to try for eleven tricks in spades, rather than accept an inadequate penalty against 5◇ doubled.

West led the ♡6, a likely singleton, and declarer won with the ace. After two rounds of trumps he played a diamond. East won and played the ♡Q, won with the king. It was no surprise when West showed out and the best chance of eleven tricks was now a loser-on-loser play in clubs.

Declarer ruffed a diamond, cashed the ace of clubs, and ruffed a club. A second diamond ruff left the lead in dummy with these cards still to be played:

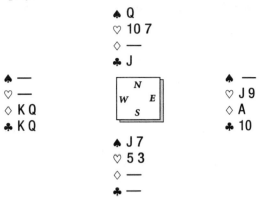

When declarer played the ♣J from dummy East could not beat the card. Declarer threw a heart loser from his hand and West had to win the trick. The ensuing minor-suit return allowed declarer to ruff in the dummy and throw the last heart from his hand. Contract made!

Key points

1. Sometimes a throw-in will assist you only when a particular defender can be thrown in. One way of achieving this is to lead a losing card that only one defender can beat. Instead of ruffing this card, you discard a loser. The gain comes when the defender thrown on lead has to give you a trick.

2. When your exit suit is something like A-K-x-x opposite x-x, only one defender can hold the four cards necessary to win the fourth round. You will ruff the third round and exit on the fourth round. With a holding such as A-K opposite J-x-x, a particular defender will have to win the third round because he holds the queen, rather than length in the suit.

A.

♠ J 7 3 2
♡ 9 6 4
◇ A Q 10 5 4
♣ 6

♣K led

```
   N
W      E
   S
```

♠ A K
♡ K 5 2
◇ K J 9 8 3
♣ A 4 2

You arrive in 5◇ after West has made a takeout double of your 1◇ opening. How will you play the hand? (Trumps are 2-1).

B.

♠ Q 9 6 5 2
♡ A
◇ A Q 6 5
♣ 7 6 3

♣10 led

```
   N
W      E
   S
```

♠ A K 7 4
♡ Q 10
◇ 9 7 2
♣ A K Q J

How will you play 6♠? (West has three trumps to East's one.)

A. Win the club lead and draw trumps. After cashing the top spades, cross to dummy with a club ruff and ruff a spade. If the queen appears, your problems are over. If not, re-enter dummy with a second club ruff and lead the ♠J, throwing a heart loser from your hand. You hope that West will hold the ♠Q and will be endplayed. If East produces the spade queen, ruff and lead a heart from the South hand. Your only remaining hope is that West will have to win the heart trick (for example, from ♡AQJ10) and will then be endplayed.

B. Win the club lead, draw trumps, and cash the ♡A. Play your remaining club winners, throwing a diamond from dummy, then lead the ♡Q. If West fails to cover, discard a diamond loser from dummy (a loser-on-loser play). When East wins with the king, he will have to lead into the diamond tenace or give you a ruff-and-discard. If West does cover the ♡Q, ruff and lead a low diamond from dummy. You will succeed when West holds the ◇K, or East has to win from ◇KJ doubleton or any holding headed by the ◇KJ10. You will succeed also when East mistakenly goes in with the king from K-x.

CHAPTER 4

Partial Eliminations

In a perfect elimination play, you draw trumps, remove all the side suits except for the key suit, then exit. Sometimes it is not possible to eliminate the suits completely. An endplay may still succeed, however, provided the defender who is thrown in has no more cards in the suit that you were unable to eliminate.

Suppose this is one of your side suits:

◇ A 9 7 2

◇ J 3 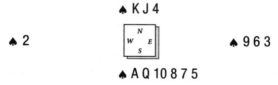 ◇ Q 10 8 4

◇ K 6 5

Cashing the ace and king does not completely eliminate the suit, since East can still safely play a diamond. If you can throw West on lead, however, this may still be productive.

Perhaps this is your trump suit:

♠ K J 4

♠ 2 ♠ 9 6 3

♠ A Q 10 8 7 5

You draw two rounds of trumps, disappointed to see the suit breaking 3-1. If you draw a third round, there will be no ruff-and-discard element in the end position. Leave one trump outstanding, however, and you may be able to throw West in to your advantage. He will not have a safe exit in trumps.

Let's see a full deal that involves this trump holding:

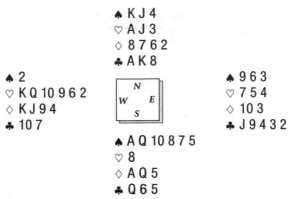

```
              ♠ K J 4
              ♡ A J 3
              ◇ 8 7 6 2
              ♣ A K 8
♠ 2                          ♠ 9 6 3
♡ K Q 10 9 6 2    N          ♡ 7 5 4
◇ K J 9 4       W   E        ◇ 10 3
♣ 10 7            S          ♣ J 9 4 3 2
              ♠ A Q 10 8 7 5
              ♡ 8
              ◇ A Q 5
              ♣ Q 6 5
```

West opens with a weak two-bid in hearts and you arrive in 6♠. You win the ♡K lead with the ace and draw two rounds of trumps with the ace and king. When West shows out on the second round, prospects for a clean-cut elimination vanish. Abandoning the trump suit for a moment, you ruff a heart in your hand, then cash three rounds of clubs successfully. The lead is in the dummy and this is the position:

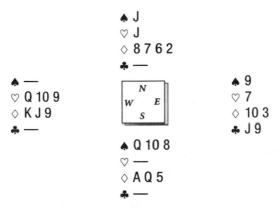

```
              ♠ J
              ♡ J
              ◇ 8 7 6 2
              ♣ —
♠ —                          ♠ 9
♡ Q 10 9        N            ♡ 7
◇ K J 9       W   E          ◇ 10 3
♣ —              S           ♣ J 9
              ♠ Q 10 8
              ♡ —
              ◇ A Q 5
              ♣ —
```

You play the ♡J and discard a diamond from hand (a loser-on-loser play). West is now on lead. It makes no difference that you have not eliminated the trump suit. West has no more trumps, so he will have to return a diamond into your tenace or play another heart. If he chooses the latter option, you will ruff with dummy's master trump and throw the ◇Q from your hand. You can then cross to the ◇A to draw the last trump and claim your contract.

You can see now why it was not advisable to draw the last trump before throwing West in. Had you done so, his heart exit would not have given you a ruff-and-discard.

Sometimes the only hope of success is that a particular defender is short in one of the side suits. By cashing whatever winners you have in that suit, you hope to exhaust his holding before you throw him in. Look at this deal:

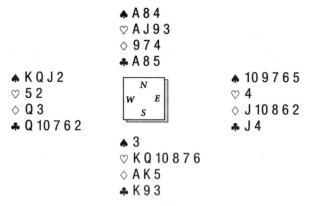

♠ A 8 4
♡ A J 9 3
◇ 9 7 4
♣ A 8 5

♠ K Q J 2
♡ 5 2
◇ Q 3
♣ Q 10 7 6 2

♠ 10 9 7 6 5
♡ 4
◇ J 10 8 6 2
♣ J 4

♠ 3
♡ K Q 10 8 7 6
◇ A K 5
♣ K 9 3

West leads the ♠K against 6♡ and you can hardly believe it when dummy goes down and the contract has so little play. A minor-suit squeeze would require one defender to hold five cards in both minors. That's extremely unlikely. A better chance (not that it's a great one) is that the defenders will hold one five-card minor each.

You ruff a spade high at trick two, cross to dummy with a trump, and ruff the remaining spade high. After drawing the last trump, you cash your top cards in the minors. These cards remain:

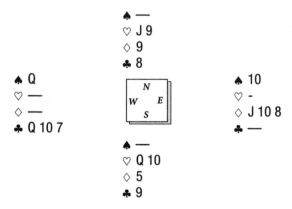

♠ —
♡ J 9
◇ 9
♣ 8

♠ Q
♡ —
◇ —
♣ Q 10 7

♠ 10
♡ -
◇ J 10 8
♣ —

♠ —
♡ Q 10
◇ 5
♣ 9

The elimination is not complete. Indeed, neither minor-suit has been eliminated. However, when you exit in either minor the defender who wins the trick will be endplayed, forced to give a ruff-and-discard.

Sometimes it is a lack of entries that prevents a complete elimination:

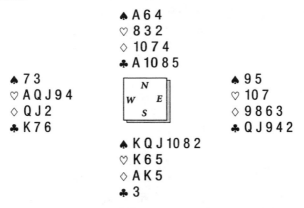

♠ A 6 4
♡ 8 3 2
◇ 10 7 4
♣ A 10 8 5

♠ 7 3
♡ A Q J 9 4
◇ Q J 2
♣ K 7 6

♠ 9 5
♡ 10 7
◇ 9 8 6 3
♣ Q J 9 4 2

♠ K Q J 10 8 2
♡ K 6 5
◇ A K 5
♣ 3

West opens 1♡ and you end in 4♠ (missing the superior spot in 3NT). West leads the ◇Q and you win with the ace. Knowing from the bidding that West holds the ♡A, you turn your mind to a possible elimination. After playing a club to the ace and ruffing a club, you cross your fingers and draw two rounds of trumps with the king and ace. Yes! The trumps are 2-2. You ruff one more club and exit with king and another diamond. The club suit is not completely eliminated, because there were only two convenient entries to dummy. No matter — West is out of clubs. When he wins the third round of diamonds he will have to give you the game-going trick.

Key points

1. Various factors may prevent you from achieving a complete elimination. The need to have a trump remaining in both hands for a potential ruff-and-discard may prevent you from drawing trumps completely. Lack of entries, or insufficient trumps, may prevent you from completely eliminating one of the side suits.

2. An elimination play may still succeed if the defender thrown on lead has no cards left in the relevant suit. Such a play is known as a 'partial elimination'.

A.

♠ A 7
♥ J 9 5 4
♦ A Q 4
♣ A 7 4 2

♠Q led

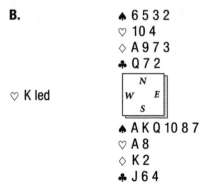

♠ K 8
♥ A K 7 6 2
♦ K 2
♣ K 9 8 3

You reach 6♥ and win the spade lead with the king. When you cash the ace and king of trumps, West shows out on the second round. Plan the play.

B.

♠ 6 5 3 2
♥ 10 4
♦ A 9 7 3
♣ Q 7 2

♥ K led

♠ A K Q 10 8 7
♥ A 8
♦ K 2
♣ J 6 4

You reach 4♠ after West has opened 1♥. West leads the ♥K. How will you play the hand?

Answers

A. If East has a singleton or doubleton club, the contract still has an excellent chance. Cash the two black aces, then lead a club towards your king. If East started with only one club, he cannot afford to ruff thin air and you will win with the club king. Next play three rounds of diamonds, throwing a club from your hand. If East ruffs one of these, he will be endplayed. If he doesn't ruff, you will throw him in with the trump queen anyway. Clubs are only partially eliminated but if East has no more clubs he will be endplayed, forced to give you a ruff-and-discard.

B. The cruel lack of entries to dummy in the trump suit prevents you from eliminating the diamond suit completely. If West has the queen and jack of hearts, which is likely after the lead, there will still be a chance to endplay him. Draw trumps, cash the king and ace of diamonds, and ruff a diamond. Exit with a heart, now. If West has to win and he has no more diamonds, he will be endplayed. He will have to open the club suit or concede a ruff-and-discard.

CHAPTER 5

The Throw-In

In this chapter we deal with endplays where the element of ruff-and-discard is absent. This may be for the very good reason that the hand is being played in notrump! In general such plays are more difficult to perform than a standard ruff-and-discard elimination. That's because you often need to read the cards quite accurately.

We start with a straightforward example of a throw-in.

```
Both Vul.            ♠ A Q 4
Dealer West          ♡ A J 3
                     ◇ Q 7 6 2
                     ♣ 8 7 2
  ♠ 10 3                              ♠ J 9 8 6 2
  ♡ Q 10 6          ┌─────────┐      ♡ 8 7 5 2
  ◇ K J 4          │    N    │      ◇ 10 9 3
  ♣ K Q J 10 4     │ W     E │      ♣ 9
                   │    S    │
                     └─────────┘
                     ♠ K 7 5
                     ♡ K 9 4
                     ◇ A 8 5
                     ♣ A 6 5 3
```

WEST	NORTH	EAST	SOUTH
1♣	pass	pass	1NT
pass	3NT	all pass	

West leads the ♣K, which you allow to win. He continues the suit and East shows out on the second round. How should you play the hand?

Only thirteen points are missing, so East will hold no more than a jack or so. You need the heart finesse to succeed, so you might as well play a heart to the jack at Trick 3. When that wins, you can count eight top tricks. A ninth will come from throwing West in with a club, forcing him to lead away from the ♢K. You cash your winners in the majors, West releasing the ♢4. This position has been reached:

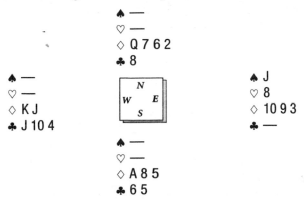

```
              ♠ —
              ♡ —
              ♢ Q 7 6 2
              ♣ 8
  ♠ —                        ♠ J
  ♡ —          ┌─────┐       ♡ 8
  ♢ K J        │  N  │       ♢ 10 9 3
  ♣ J 10 4     │ W   E│      ♣ —
               │  S  │
               └─────┘
              ♠ —
              ♡ —
              ♢ A 8 5
              ♣ 6 5
```

Now you throw West in with a club. He scores three more tricks in the suit, bringing the defenders' total to four, but at Trick 12 he has to play a diamond. You rise with dummy's ♢Q and the game is made.

As you see, the element of elimination was still present. You had to remove West's major suits, thereby forcing him to play a diamond after scoring his club tricks. On the next deal it is not so automatic to read the cards unless the defenders assist you.

Neither Vul.
Dealer South

```
                    ♠ A 7 4
                    ♡ K J 5
                    ♢ Q J 8 3
                    ♣ K 7 2
  ♠ 8 3                           ♠ J 10 9 6
  ♡ 8 7 3          ┌─────┐        ♡ Q 10 9 2
  ♢ 7 6 2          │  N  │        ♢ 10 9 5
  ♣ Q 10 9 8 4     │ W   E│       ♣ J 3
                   │  S  │
                   └─────┘
                    ♠ K Q 5 2
                    ♡ A 6 4
                    ♢ A K 4
                    ♣ A 6 5
```

WEST	NORTH	EAST	SOUTH
			2NT
pass	6NT	all pass	

West leads the ◇6 and you play four rounds of diamonds immediately, throwing a club from the South hand. Suppose first that East chooses to discard a club. Three rounds of spades will reveal the 4-2 break and two rounds of clubs will complete your count on the hand. You can exit with the fourth spade, in the certain knowledge that East will have to return a heart into dummy's tenace.

What if East throws a heart instead of a club on the fourth round of diamonds? Now the situation is not so certain. You cash three spades and two clubs, as before, but this time East does not show out on the second round of clubs. You now have to guess. If East started with four hearts and two clubs, a spade throw-in will succeed. If East started with three hearts and ♣QJx, an attempted throw-in would result in two black-suit losers. You must guess whether to finesse West for the ♡Q or to throw East in.

A defender who can see a potential throw-in approaching will often be devious with his discards. For example, he might throw the nine from ♡Q1092 to create the illusion that he has unguarded the queen. Declarer should look just as carefully at the discards of the other defender. He may well give away the crucial information, particularly when it is the partnership's normal practice to signal distribution.

Many throw-ins occur after a defender has been forced to discard one or more winning cards. This is a typical deal:

East-West Vul.
Dealer West

♠ Q 10 5 2
♡ J 5
◇ K Q 4
♣ Q 6 5 3

♠ A K
♡ K Q 10 7 4 3
◇ 6 5
♣ K 8 4

                N
            W   E
                S

♠ 9 7 6 4 3
♡ 9 2
◇ 10 2
♣ J 10 7 2

♠ J 8
♡ A 8 6
◇ A J 9 8 7 3
♣ A 9

WEST	NORTH	EAST	SOUTH
1♡	pass	pass	2◇
pass	3◇	pass	3NT
all pass			

West leads the ♡K and you hold up the ace until the third round of the suit. At this stage West has made two tricks and has five more winners in his hand. However, when you run the diamonds he has to find four discards. To keep a guard on his ♣K, he will have to throw one low club and three major-suit winners.

Suppose West throws all his hearts. It will be obvious now for you to exit in spades, forcing West to lead from the ♣K at Trick 12. West does better to bare the ♣K and throw two heart winners. Now you will have to guess whether he holds ♠A ♡10 ♣Kx (when a throw-in will work), or ♠AK ♡10 ♣K (when you must cash the ace of clubs).

Occasionally, the intention behind a throw-in is to reach winners in a dummy to which there is no entry. On the next deal the throw-in itself costs a trick. However, the defender thrown in has to surrender two tricks in return, so it is still good business.

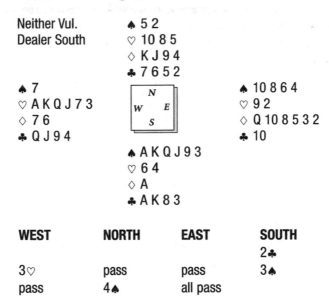

Neither Vul.
Dealer South

	♠ 5 2	
	♡ 10 8 5	
	◇ K J 9 4	
	♣ 7 6 5 2	
♠ 7		♠ 10 8 6 4
♡ A K Q J 7 3		♡ 9 2
◇ 7 6		◇ Q 10 8 5 3 2
♣ Q J 9 4		♣ 10
	♠ A K Q J 9 3	
	♡ 6 4	
	◇ A	
	♣ A K 8 3	

WEST	NORTH	EAST	SOUTH
			2♣
3♡	pass	pass	3♠
pass	4♠	all pass	

West plays three top hearts. East throws the ♣10 on the third round and you ruff. Is that all that needs to be said? No, you must ruff with the nine! If East's ♣10 is a singleton, you have two club losers. Even at this early stage you must foresee an endplay on East. Your lowest trump will be required as a throw-in card.

You play three rounds of trumps, discovering the 4-1 break, and continue with the ◇A and the ♣A. Seeing that he will have to lead into dummy's diamond tenace if he ruffs, East discards a diamond. You throw him in with the ♠3 on the next trick, however, and dispose of your two club losers on the enforced diamond return.

Suppose the ♠4 and the ♠3 had been interchanged. An alert East could defeat the game by retaining the ♠3 as his last trump and refusing to accept your Greek gift of a trump trick!

Key points

1. A throw-in can be more difficult to perform than a ruff-and-discard elimination, because you may need to read the cards accurately.

2. You can often put a defender under pressure by cashing side-suit winners. To retain a guard such as K-x, he may have to discard winners of his own. He will then be susceptible to a throw-in.

A.

    ♠ Q 8 3
    ♡ 9 4
    ◇ 10 8 2
    ♣ A K J 6 5

◇ K led

      N
   W   E
      S

    ♠ A J 4
    ♡ A Q 6
    ◇ A 9 4
    ♣ Q 8 7 2

West leads the ◇K against your contract of 3NT. How will you play the hand? If you duck, West will continue with the ◇Q and East

B.

    ♠ 6 5 4
    ♡ J 7 6
    ◇ Q 10 6 2
    ♣ K 9 7

♣A led

      N
   W   E
      S

    ♠ A K Q 7 2
    ♡ A K 5
    ◇ A K
    ♣ 8 6 2

WEST	NORTH	EAST	SOUTH
3♣	pass	pass	double
pass	3◇	pass	4♠
all pass			

will follow suit.

West leads the ♣A against your 4♠ contract, East throwing a heart. The ♣Q is covered and ruffed, East returning a trump. Plan the play.

C.

♠ 8 5
♡ 9 7 6 2
◇ A K 5
♣ Q 9 7 2

♠K led

♠ A 10 2
♡ A K 4
◇ Q J 9 4
♣ A 5 3

WEST	NORTH	EAST	SOUTH
			1◇
1♠	dbl	pass	2NT
pass	3NT	all pass	

West leads the spade king against your 3NT contract, East playing the seven to suggest a doubleton spade. Plan the play.

D.

♠ A Q 6
♡ A Q 4 3
◇ A Q 6 2
♣ 6 2

♣9 led

♠ 9 8 3
♡ 10 7 2
◇ K J 9 4
♣ A J 3

WEST	NORTH	EAST	SOUTH
		1♣	pass
pass	dbl	pass	1NT
pass	3NT	all pass	

West leads the ♣9 to East's queen. Plan the play. (Clubs are 6-2, as indicated by the opening lead.)

Answers

A. You should win the second diamond and play two or three rounds of clubs, removing West's safe exit in that suit. You then exit with a diamond. After cashing at most two more winners in the suit (you will discard one spade and one heart), West will have to lead into a major-suit tenace.

It would not be a good idea to play five rounds of clubs before performing the throw-in. You would then have no convenient discards from the South hand when West cashed his diamonds.

B. You must hope that East started with four trumps and can be thrown in. Win the trump switch and draw a second round of trumps, West showing out. Cash $\diamond$ AK and $\heartsuit$ A, then play the $\spadesuit$ 2 to East's last trump, surrendering an unnecessary trump trick. A diamond return will give you ten tricks. If East plays a heart instead, you must run it to the jack, hoping that East holds the $\heartsuit$ Q.

C. The best chance is to find West with the $\clubsuit$ K and to throw him in to lead away from this card. Win the second round of spades and cash your six winners in the red suits. To retain a guard on his $\clubsuit$ K, West will have to discard a spade winner. You can then throw him with a third round of spades. If West keeps all his spades, preventing a throw-in, cash the $\clubsuit$ A in the hope that the king will fall.

D. You should duck the club lead and win the club continuation with the jack. (If East switches to a diamond at Trick 2, you will win in dummy and finesse the $\clubsuit$ J yourself.) Next cash all your minor-suit winners. East almost certainly holds both major-suit kings. If he retains only two club winners, he will have to reduce himself to K-x in both majors or to unguard one of the kings. Play ace and another of the major in which you judge East to be shorter. Unless you have misread the cards and East still has K-x-x in this suit (having unguarded the other king), you will make the contract. He will have to lead from the other king at Trick 12.

If instead East retains all three club winners, he must have unguarded one of the kings. Cash both the major-suit aces and wait for the bare king to tumble!

Defending Eliminations and Throw-Ins

In this chapter we will see how you can thwart an attempted elimination or throw-in. Even when there is no sure-fire defense, you can often put declarer to a guess. Make him work for his contract!

Do not assist in the elimination process

Once you understand the mechanics of elimination play from declarer's point of view, you are most of the way towards understanding how to defend again it. Declarer needs to eliminate one or more of the side suits? Very well, you must refuse to assist him in this process.

West was much too helpful when this first deal was played:

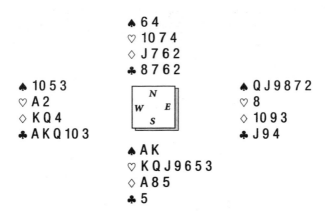

                        ♠ 6 4
                        ♡ 10 7 4
                        ◇ J 7 6 2
                        ♣ 8 7 6 2
    ♠ 10 5 3   ♠ Q J 9 8 7 2
    ♡ A 2   ♡ 8
    ◇ K Q 4   ◇ 10 9 3
    ♣ A K Q 10 3   ♣ J 9 4
                        ♠ A K
                        ♡ K Q J 9 6 5 3
                        ◇ A 8 5
                        ♣ 5

South played in 4♡ after West had opened 1♣. West led the king of clubs and East's ♣4 showed an odd number of cards in the suit. When West continued with another high club. Declarer ruffed and led a low trump. West was too mean to expend his ace and dummy's ten won the trick. Declarer ruffed another club, then cashed the two spade winners. West had to win the next trump with the bare ace. He could not afford to play on diamonds, so he was forced to assist declarer's elimination further, playing another club. Declarer ruffed in the South hand and surveyed this end position:

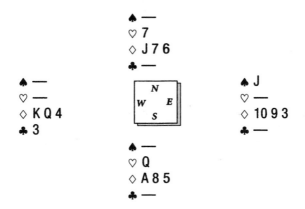

                        ♠ —
                        ♡ 7
                        ◇ J 7 6
                        ♣ —
    ♠ —   ♠ J
    ♡ —   ♡ —
    ◇ K Q 4   ◇ 10 9 3
    ♣ 3   ♣ —
                        ♠ —
                        ♡ Q
                        ◇ A 8 5
                        ♣ —

Now came the dénouement, a diamond towards the jack. West, deservedly on this occasion, was endplayed. After winning with one of his diamond honors he had to lead from the other honor or concede a ruff-and-discard.

....

Chapter 6 - Defending Eliminations and Throw-Ins • **45**

West helped declarer no fewer than three times on this deal. Declarer had nowhere near enough entries to dummy to eliminate the clubs himself. Had West not assisted in the process, he would have had a safe club exit later in the play.

Retaining an exit card

When there is risk that you will be caught in an elimination ending, you must be careful to retain a safe exit card. West failed to heed such advice on this deal:

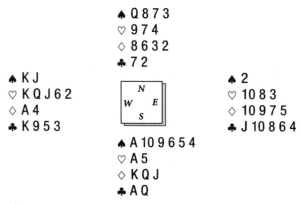

```
              ♠ Q 8 7 3
              ♡ 9 7 4
              ◇ 8 6 3 2
              ♣ 7 2
  ♠ K J                        ♠ 2
  ♡ K Q J 6 2                  ♡ 10 8 3
  ◇ A 4                        ◇ 10 9 7 5
  ♣ K 9 5 3                    ♣ J 10 8 6 4
              ♠ A 10 9 6 5 4
              ♡ A 5
              ◇ K Q J
              ♣ A Q
```

South played in 4♠ after West had opened 1♡. West's king of hearts was allowed to win the first trick, East signaling with the three to indicate an odd number of cards in the suit. Declarer won the second round of hearts and noted that he had a potential loser in each of the four suits. A 3-3 diamond break might come to his rescue. Another possibility was to endplay West.

The king of diamonds was led at Trick 3. West won with the ace and the critical moment of the hand had been reached. Suppose you had held the West cards. What would you have played next?

Not giving the matter much thought, West exited 'safely' with another heart. This is what declarer had wanted to see. He ruffed in the South hand and cashed the ace of trumps, both defenders following. He then played the queen and jack of diamonds. If West ruffed the third diamond, he would be endplayed — forced to lead a club or to concede a ruff-and-discard. He chose to discard instead but was thrown in with a trump on the next trick anyway. Contract made!

West had a safe exit in hearts and should not have squandered this early in the play. Had he exited with a diamond when he won with the diamond ace, he would have had a safe heart exit card when thrown in later.

Unblocking honor cards to avoid a throw-in

Suppose you are sitting West and declarer (South) has a side suit like this:

If you follow with low cards when he cashes the ace and king, you may find yourself thrown in on the third round. You can avoid this predicament by playing your queen under one of declarer's honors. This is not so risky as it may seem. If declarer held ◇AKJ he would doubtless have taken a finesse in the suit. In any case, if there is a throw-in staring you in the face, your only counter may be to unblock and hope that partner holds the jack

Let's see a full deal based on this situation.

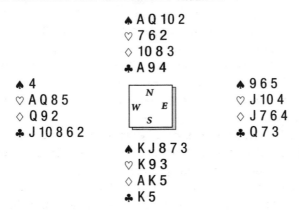

South plays in 4♠ and, sitting West, you lead the ♣J. Declarer wins with the king, draws trumps in three rounds, and cashes the ace and king of diamonds. If the ◇Q is still in your hand, you will regret it! Declarer will eliminate the club suit and endplay you with a third round of diamonds.

With declarer still holding trumps in both hands, the risk of an elimination is evident. If you unblock the ◇Q under declarer's king, East will be able to win the third round of diamonds. A heart switch through declarer's king will then defeat the contract.

Take the West seat again on this deal:

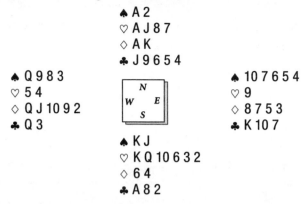

♠ A 2
♡ A J 8 7
◇ A K
♣ J 9 6 5 4

♠ Q 9 8 3
♡ 5 4
◇ Q J 10 9 2
♣ Q 3

♠ 10 7 6 5 4
♡ 9
◇ 8 7 5 3
♣ K 10 7

♠ K J
♡ K Q 10 6 3 2
◇ 6 4
♣ A 8 2

South opens 1♡ and is soon in 6♡. He wins your diamond lead in the dummy, crosses to the ♣A, and leads the ♡K. Is the ♣Q still in your hand? If so, declarer will make the slam. He will draw a second round of trumps, eliminate spades and diamonds, then lead a club. When you win with the queen, you will have to give him a ruff-and-discard. Partner cannot rescue you by overtaking with the king, since dummy's jack would then be set up.

The remedy, as before, is to play your dangerous card — here the ♣Q — under declarer's winner. Partner can then score two club tricks when declarer exits in the suit.

Note that it was clever of declarer to play a club at Trick 2, perhaps seeming to be crossing to hand for a trump finesse. Had he drawn trumps first, the risk of an endplay would have been more obvious.

Sometimes the defenders have no counter. Suppose on the last deal that the clubs had been:

♣ J 9 6 5 4

♣ Q 10 3

♣ K 7

♣ A 8 2

East cannot afford to unblock the king because declarer simply leads up to the ♣J if he does. There is no escape from the endplay.

Cashing winning cards to avoid a throw-in

When you hold a doubleton ace or king in a side suit, it can be important to take the honor on the first round. If you play low instead, you risk being thrown in. West fell into such a trap on this deal:

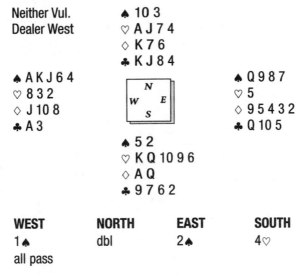

Neither Vul.
Dealer West

	♠ 10 3	
	♡ A J 7 4	
	◇ K 7 6	
	♣ K J 8 4	
♠ A K J 6 4		♠ Q 9 8 7
♡ 8 3 2		♡ 5
◇ J 10 8		◇ 9 5 4 3 2
♣ A 3		♣ Q 10 5
	♠ 5 2	
	♡ K Q 10 9 6	
	◇ A Q	
	♣ 9 7 6 2	

WEST	NORTH	EAST	SOUTH
1♠	dbl	2♠	4♡
all pass			

West cashed two rounds of spades, then switched to the ◇J. Declarer won with the ace and drew trumps in three rounds. He then cashed the ◇Q and led a small club from the South hand. West knew that his side needed two club tricks to beat the contract. Thinking no further, he produced a smooth low card.

Declarer now needed to read the cards accurately. Had West started with ◇J8 ♣AQ3, when a finesse of ♣J would succeed? Or did he hold ◇J108 ♣A3? Declarer reasoned that the ◇J switch would have been unnecessarily dangerous from ◇J8, particularly when West had a safe trump exit. He therefore placed West with ◇J108. 'King of clubs, please,' he said.

Declarer threw a club on the king of diamonds, then led a club to West's bare ace. A ruff-and-discard ensued and away went South's last club loser. Contract made.

West should have risen with the ♣A on the first round of the suit. He could then have exited safely in clubs, allowing partner to score the eventual setting trick with the ♣Q.

There are many similar positions. Suppose declarer has eliminated the other suits and you need three club tricks to beat the contract here:

♣ 10 9 3

♣ A 6 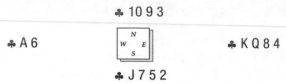 ♣ K Q 8 4

♣ J 7 5 2

When declarer leads a low club from his hand, you must be there with your ace. The same medicine is appropriate here:

♣ 10 9 3

♣ A Q 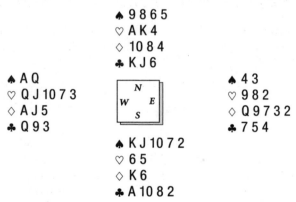 ♣ K J 8 6 4

♣ 7 5 2

You must rise with the ace and play the queen.

Imagine now that in the last two positions North was declarer and South the dummy. Of course you would have to make exactly the same play, ace on the first round.

Many a contract is surrendered when defenders are thrown in with a bare trump honor. West was asleep when this deal was played:

♠ 9 8 6 5
♡ A K 4
◇ 10 8 4
♣ K J 6

♠ A Q
♡ Q J 10 7 3
◇ A J 5
♣ Q 9 3

♠ 4 3
♡ 9 8 2
◇ Q 9 7 3 2
♣ 7 5 4

♠ K J 10 7 2
♡ 6 5
◇ K 6
♣ A 10 8 2

South played in 4♠ after West had opened 1♡. Declarer won the ♡Q lead in dummy and ran the ♠9 to West's queen. Giving the matter insufficient thought, West continued with the ♡J. Declarer won with the king, crossed to the ♣A and took a successful finesse against West's club queen. He then eliminated hearts and clubs and exited with a trump to the bare ace. This was the position, with West on lead:

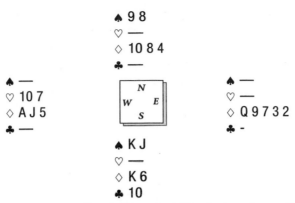

A heart would give a ruff-and-discard, so West had to play on diamonds, setting up South's king. Suppose West had defended more sensibly when he won the trump queen, cashing the ♠A and exiting safely in hearts. Declarer would then have had no way to avoid two further losers in diamonds.

Holding up an ace in the elimination position

Suppose declarer has eliminated trumps and two of the side suits. He now plays on the third suit, where you will need two tricks to beat the contract. You must be wary of taking an ace on the first round, in case this leaves you endplayed. This is the type of deal we have in mind:

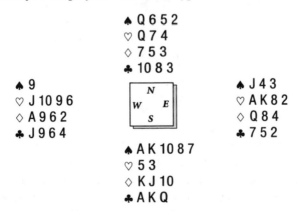

South plays in 4♠ and you lead the ♡J. Declarer ruffs the third round of hearts and draws two rounds of trumps with the ace and king. He then cashes three club winners and crosses to dummy with the trump queen. At this stage, with all suits except diamonds eliminated, he plays a diamond to the jack. Over to you.

If you win with the ace, you will have to return a diamond into the K-10 or concede a ruff-and-discard. Allow the jack to win and declarer is powerless. He will have to lead away from his tenace and the defenders will score two diamond tricks to defeat the contract.

There are many similar positions:

$\diamond$ 10 7 3

$\diamond$ A J 5   N W E S $\diamond$ 9 8 6 2

$\diamond$ K Q 4

Declarer sets up an elimination position, then plays a diamond to the king or queen. West must duck.

Look at this position, too:

$\diamond$ 10 8 3

$\diamond$ A 9 5   N W E S $\diamond$ J 7 6 2

$\diamond$ K Q 4

Again West must hold up the ace, or declarer will have a winning option on the $\diamond$ 5 return.

Sometimes the smooth duck of an ace will give declarer a losing option:

$\diamond$ 8 7 3

$\diamond$ A 5 2   N W E S $\diamond$ J 9 6 4

$\diamond$ K Q 10

If you win with the ace, your enforced diamond return will make life easy for declarer. Play low, without considering the matter, and he will have a difficult guess on the next round.

Discarding to give declarer a guess

When you are threatened with a throw-in, you can often present declarer with a guess. The most common situation occurs when you have a known number of winners in your hand and may or may not have a guarded honor accompanying them. That's the case here:

```
Neither Vul.          ♠ 9 5
Dealer East           ♡ A J 8 2
                      ◇ K 10 9 3
                      ♣ A Q 4
♠ 10 4                                    ♠ K Q J 8 7 3 2
♡ 10 9 6 4       ┌─────────┐              ♡ 7 3
◇ 6 2            │    N    │              ◇ 8 5
♣ J 9 6 3 2      │  W   E  │              ♣ K 7
                 │    S    │
                 └─────────┘
                      ♠ A 6
                      ♡ K Q 5
                      ◇ A Q J 7 4
                      ♣ 10 8 5
```

WEST	NORTH	EAST	SOUTH
		3♠	3NT
pass	6NT	all pass	

West leads the ♠10, East overtaking with the jack. Declarer wins immediately, seeing that there will be a chance of throwing East in later, with a second round of spades.

Declarer cashes nine winners in the red suits and East must find five discards. What will happen if he retains ♣K7 and one spade winner? He might as well throw in the towel! With no guess to make, declarer will exit with a spade, certain to make the contract.

The only chance of beating the contract is for East to bare the ♣K, retaining two spade winners. Now declarer has to guess who holds the ♣K; he will have to work for his contract.

Relatively few defenders are capable of baring a king; even fewer can do so without giving the position away. It follows that you are likely to strike gold if you can master the technique yourself. Don't leave the key discard until last. On this deal, for example, East can see fairly soon that he will have to make five discards. He should throw the ♣7 early in the play.

When declarer does not have a count on the hand, the defenders have plenty of scope for deceptive discarding. For example, you might discard the ♠Q from ♠ KQ9, giving the impression that your king is now bare. That's what East does here:

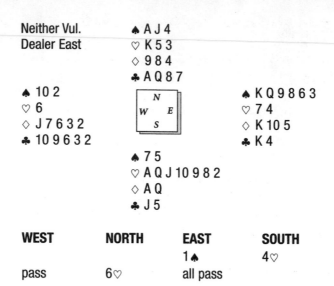

Neither Vul.
Dealer East

```
              ♠ A J 4
              ♡ K 5 3
              ♢ 9 8 4
              ♣ A Q 8 7
♠ 10 2                              ♠ K Q 9 8 6 3
♡ 6              N                  ♡ 7 4
♢ J 7 6 3 2    W   E                ♢ K 10 5
♣ 10 9 6 3 2      S                 ♣ K 4
              ♠ 7 5
              ♡ A Q J 10 9 8 2
              ♢ A Q
              ♣ J 5
```

WEST	NORTH	EAST	SOUTH
		1♠	4♡
pass	6♡	all pass	

Take the East cards. Your opening bid has told declarer that you hold nearly all of the missing high cards. He wins the ♠10 lead with the ace, draws trumps with the ace and king, then takes a successful diamond finesse. He now runs the remainder of his trump suit. How should you discard?

As soon as partner shows out on the second trump, you know how many discards you will have to find. The best idea is to throw the ♣4 fairly early and to come down to: ♠ KQ9 ♣K. When the last trump is played, throw the ♠Q. If declarer places the ♠9 with your partner, he may now throw you in, hoping for a lead into the club tenace. Note that it was important to keep precisely the ♠9 as your second spade. If you had let declarer catch sight of that, he would know that the ♠10 lead was a doubleton and would therefore have a count on your hand.

Play the right card when thrown in

Sometimes you cannot avoid being thrown in and must seek the best way to avoid losing a trick subsequently. Suppose you are West and have been forced to open this suit:

```
              ♢ A J 6
♢ K 10 5        N
              W   E            ♢ Q 8 4 2
                S
              ♢ 9 7 3
```

If you exit with the ◇5 declarer may run this to his ◇9, scoring a second trick in the suit. Exit with the ◇K instead and you save a trick.

Take the East holding here, again in an elimination position:

◇ 10 7 4

◇ A J 9 2   [N W E S]   ◇ Q 8 4

◇ K 6 3

Declarer cannot possibly go wrong if you play one of your spot-cards. Play the queen instead and he will have to guess correctly. If you hold the queen and jack, he must hold up his king, forcing you to lead from the jack on the next round.

The useless ruff-and-discard

In some positions it does not cost a trick to concede a ruff-and-discard. This is most frequently the case when declarer's key side suit lies like this:

♣ A 7 4 2

♣ Q 10 5   [N W E S]   ♣ 9 6

♣ K J 8 3

If West plays a club, it will cost a trick. If instead he concedes a ruff-and-discard, declarer will only be able to discard the fourth club from one or other hand — no use to him at all.

You can detect this situation only by counting the hand and diagnosing declarer's remaining cards. Let's look at a complete deal, from West's viewpoint:

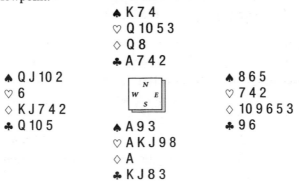

     ♠ K 7 4
     ♡ Q 10 5 3
     ◇ Q 8
     ♣ A 7 4 2

♠ Q J 10 2   ♠ 8 6 5
♡ 6   [N W E S]   ♡ 7 4 2
◇ K J 7 4 2   ◇ 10 9 6 5 3
♣ Q 10 5   ♣ 9 6

     ♠ A 9 3
     ♡ A K J 9 8
     ◇ A
     ♣ K J 8 3

South plays in 6♡ and you lead the ♠Q. Declarer wins with the ace and cashes the ♦A. He then draws trumps in three rounds and ruffs the diamond queen. Finally, he plays king and another spade, throwing you on lead. What should you do now?

You have a certain count on declarer's hand. He started with three spades, five hearts, and one diamond. So, he holds four clubs and a ruff-and-discard will not assist him. Exit with a spade or a diamond and you will eventually score the setting trick in clubs.

There is another situation where giving a ruff-and-discard is the defender's best option. Suppose you are West in this end position:

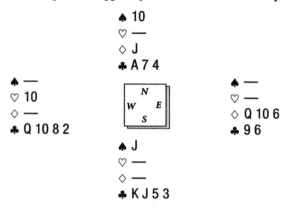

```
                    ♠ 10
                    ♡ —
                    ♦ J
                    ♣ A 7 4
    ♠ —                             ♠ —
    ♡ 10          ┌─────────┐       ♡ —
    ♦ —          │ N        │      ♦ Q 10 6
    ♣ Q 10 8 2   │ W     E  │      ♣ 9 6
                 │    S     │
                 └─────────┘
                    ♠ J
                    ♡ —
                    ♦ —
                    ♣ K J 5 3
```

Spades are trumps and you have just been thrown in (with the trump queen, say). If you play a club declarer will face his hand and claim the contract. Give a ruff-and-discard and declarer will score only four tricks: two top clubs and two trumps, scored separately.

Key points

1. Do not assist declarer in eliminating side suits. Once you have taken the available tricks in a suit, it may be better to switch elsewhere.

2. Be careful to retain your safe exit cards. If you waste them early in the play, you may find yourself endplayed later.

3. You can often avoid being endplayed by unblocking honor cards under declarer's honors. You aim to let partner win the throw-in trick rather than yourself.

4. Be particularly wary when you hold a side-suit doubleton honor. If an elimination position is threatened, it will often be right to play your honor on the first round.

QUIZ

A.

	♠ K Q 5 4
	♡ K
	◇ A 10 8 7 6 4
	♣ J 9

```
              ♠ A J 8
    N         ♡ 9 5 3
  W   E       ◇ J 5
    S         ♣ 8 6 5 4 2
```

WEST	NORTH	EAST	SOUTH
			1NT (15-17)
3♡	dbl	4♡	5◇
pass	6◇	all pass	

Partner's ♡Q lead is won in dummy. Declarer draws trumps (partner has none), cashes the ♡A, and ruffs a heart. The ♣AK are followed by the ♠6 to West's two and dummy's king. How will you defend?

B.

```
              ♠ K 8
              ♡ J 7 6 3 2
              ◇ A 9 7 2
              ♣ K 7
♠ Q J 10 2      N
♡ Q 10 5     W    E
◇ Q J 5         S
♣ 10 6 5
```

WEST	NORTH	EAST	SOUTH
			1♡
pass	3NT	pass	6♡
all pass			

North's 3NT shows a sound raise to game with no side-suit singleton. You lead the ♠Q, won by South's ace. When he plays the ace of trumps, East discards a club. Declarer cashes the king of trumps, followed by the ♠K and the king and ace of clubs. He then throws you in with your trump winner. What will you do now?

Chapter 6 - Defending Eliminations and Throw-Ins • **57**

Answers

A. The deal is from the final of the 2000 Venice Cup, between the USA and the Netherlands. If declarer held another club she would have ruffed it. Her shape must therefore be 3-3-5-2. If you capture the ♠K you will have to return a spade and declarer will make the contract if she holds the ♠10. To beat the contract for sure, you must allow the ♠K to win. Verbeek, the Dutch East, found this defense to defeat the American slam.

B. If declarer had any further card in the black suits, he would have ruffed it before throwing you in. His shape is therefore 2-5-4-2. It follows that a ruff-and-discard will not assist him. You should exit in one of the black suits. If instead you exit with a diamond honor, he may make the contract when he holds ◇K10xx.

More Bridge Titles from Master Point Press

Classic Kantar *A collection of bridge humor* by Eddie Kantar
192pp., PB   Can $19.95   US $14.95
Competitive Bidding in the 21st Century by Marshall Miles
254pp.,PB   Can. $22.95   US. $16.95

Countdown to Winning Bridge by Tim Bourke and Marc Smith
92pp., PB   Can $19.95   US $14.95

Easier Done Than Said *Brilliancy at the Bridge Table*
by Prakash K. Paranjape
128pp., PB   Can $15.95   US $12.95

For Love or Money *The Life of a Bridge Journalist*
by Mark Horton and Brian Senior (Foreword by Omar Sharif)
189pp., PB   Can $22.95   US $16.95

I Shot my Bridge Partner by Matthew Granovetter
384pp., PB   Can $19.95   US $14.95

Murder at the Bridge Table by Matthew Granovetter
320pp., PB   Can $19.95   US $14.95

Partnership Bidding *A Workbook* by Mary Paul
96pp., PB   Can $9.95   US $7.95

Playing With The Bridge Legends by Barnet Shenkin
(forewords by Zia and Michael Rosenberg)
192pp., PB   Can $22.95   US $16.95

Saints and Sinners: *The St. Titus Bridge Challenge*
by David Bird & Tim Bourke
192pp., PB   Can $19.95   US $14.95

Tales out of School 'Bridge 101' *and other stories* by David Silver
(foreword by Dorothy Hayden Truscott)
128pp., PB   Can $ 12.95   US $9.95

The Bridge Player's Bedside Book edited by Tony Forrester
256pp., HC   Can $27.95   US $19.95

The Complete Book of BOLS Bridge Tips edited by Sally Brock
176pp., PB (photographs)   Can $24.95   US$17.95

There Must Be A Way... *52 challenging bridge hands*
by Andrew Diosy (foreword by Eddie Kantar)
96pp., PB $9.95 US & Can.

You Have to See This... *52 more challenging bridge problems*
by Andrew Diosy and Linda Lee
96pp., PB   Can $12.95   US $9.95

World Class — *Conversations with the Bridge Masters* by Marc Smith
288pp., PB (photographs)   Can $24.95   US $17.95